MW01252619

VISA GOLD
WELCOMES YOU TO TORONTO

CONCEPT AND CREATIVE DIRECTION CHRISTINA TEMPLE

DESIGN AND CREATIVE DIRECTION DAVID CHRISTIAN

DESIGN ASSISTANCE + MUSIC SEAN WATSON ———————————————————

TEXT DAVID CHRISTIAN AND CHRISTINA TEMPLE

COVER PHOTOGRAPHY RON FEHLING

SW

FIRST PUBLISHED IN CANADA BY BEAT DESIGN INC.

80 SPADINA AVENUE, STUDIO 304, TORONTO CANADA M5V 2J3

PRINTED IN CANADA BY WOOD PRINTING AND GRAPHICS INCORPORATED

COPYRIGHT © 1997 CHRISTINA TEMPLE AND DAVID CHRISTIAN

All rights reserved. No part of this publication may be reproduced,
stored in a retrieval system, or transmitted in any form or by any
means, electronic, mechanical, photocopying, recording or otherwise,
without prior permission of the publishers.

ISBN 0-9681996-0-7 SOFT COVER

ISBN 0-9681966-1-5 HARD COVER

CATALOGUING IN PUBLICATION DATA IS AVAILABLE FROM THE NATIONAL LIBRARY OF CANADA

A PORTION OF THE SALES OF BEAT TORONTO WILL BE GIVEN TO CANFAR TO HELP FIGHT AIDS

CONTENTS

TIME:OUT

Time to spend in the company of an interesting friend. In the company of interesting strangers. Where to go? Heard any good restaurants lately? Ready to take a chance? Do you feel lucky? Beat. Information, entertainment, as enjoyable as your evening out. A guide to our city that really shows you the way. You've never seen one quite like this before. Guaranteed. Fifty of Toronto's most interesting restaurants. One hundred of Toronto's most interesting pages. Each spread, the reflection of a sensibility A different point of view. A different attitude. Beat.   Made you look!

Toronto enjoys an undisputed reputation as one of North America's great food cities. Establishments in abundance where the creative spirit is not confined to the kitchen but flows out to the street. Beat Toronto celebrates these spaces and this attitude.

We are a visual guide, a souvenir, a catalogue of Toronto's restaurant scene. Our city deserves a book that salutes this spirit with the same energy and passion. Noodles, Cibo, Fenton's, The Courtyard Café — some of Toronto's legendary restaurants, some of your finest experiences have passed into memory. Memories are wonderful but imprecise. No one documented these establishments while there was still time. So much creativity has no permanent marker. Until now.

Restaurants are our social theatres. One sign of maturity, characteristic of a cosmopolitan metropolis is the level of sophistication and variety of a city's restaurants. Young towns don't have them, small towns won't have many. We do.

Toronto boasts such wonderful blended neighbourhoods, different people living side by side, not divided into separate, hostile territories. Take a walk through the Annex or a stroll along Queen West.

Then there are neighbourhoods where one culture is dominant. China Town, Little Italy, North Toronto. Each culture, another ingredient in the recipe, another dish on the table. Beat Toronto wants to take you to these neighbourhoods to sample, to taste, to enjoy. From fine dining to diner, bar to bistro, rock bottom prices to financial indulgence.

No one paid to be in this book so we were free to select the offbeat and small scale along with the upscale and well known. We have tried to keep our choices democratic. To some of you there will be glaring omissions and perhaps some mystifying selections. All we can say is . . . "Volume 2"

Pick up a traditional restaurant guide and you are presented with a generic shot of the empty dining room. Perhaps a mug shot of the owners and chef. **Now we know why.**

We decided at the outset to adopt a more personal, intimate point of view, focusing on the details, the gestures, whether the work of highly skilled designers or inventive owner operators. Whenever possible we wanted to shoot live. We were privileged to be allowed into the kitchens, behind the lines, and in the way and we want to thank everyone on staff for their cooperation.

Excuse me, oh sorry. Click. Whatever else can be said about restaurant lighting, it certainly isn't camera-friendly. It is to the enormous credit of the photographers, given such chaos that they captured so much of our vision and expanded it as well.

Beat began at the Bovine Sex Club, the choice of our first recruit, Chris Gordaneer and ended at The Horseshoe Tavern with Anthony Cheung, (two places not noted for their cuisine but nourishing nonetheless). In between, George Simhoni contributed his quiet elegance, Tom Feiler his brilliant sense of colour, Ian Campbell his detailed eye. Frank Hoedl's skill with black and white provided counterpoint as did Kathryn Hollinrake with her gentle vision. Ed Chin gave us his fresh, youthful eye, and Ron Fehling also known as "Mr. Location", slipped effortlessly between the tables.

"We're asking for a leap of faith."

We would like to thank the corporate sponsors and the corporate people who helped finance this venture. They are all, in some way, associated with this great industry.

Charles S. Coffey and Beverly A. MacAdam for great support at Royal Bank.

Glenn N. Smith at Gilbey Canada Inc.

Paul Cooke at Labatt Breweries of Canada

Michael and Peter Sainsbury at Sainsbury & Company Limited

Great Brands of Europe for our Evian

Salvatore Costanzo at Illy Espresso Canada Inc.

Donald J.P. Ziraldo at Inniskillin Wines Inc.

Peter M. Brenzel and his team at Wood Printing and Graphics Inc.

Chris Whalen and the creatives at Stafford Graphics

Few people realize their dreams.
I have

To my Father, Mother, Sister, and
Nana for their love and support.
David Christian for his patience.
Sean Watson for his youthful spirit.
Lori Heath, my best friend.
Donald Ziraldo, my mentor.
Charlie Coffey for his wisdom.
Peter Brenzel, a true friend.
George Simhoni, a believer.
Ron Fehling, a calming force.
Bob Humphrey for his perseverance.

Thanks
Christopher

PLATES

1 BLACK & BLUE ○○○
2 ENOTECA ○○○
3 SOTTO VOCE ○○
4 NORTH 44° ○○○
5 SWATOW ○
6 GRANO ○
7 MESSIS ○○
8 KIT KAT ○○
9 CENTRO ○○○
10 LETTIERI ¢
11 CANOE ○○○
12 MERCER STREET GRILL ○○○
13 XANGÔ ○○
14 NAMI ○○
15 EIGENSINN FARM ○○○
16 RODNEY'S OYSTER HOUSE ○○
17 LOLITA'S LUST ○○
18 PAN ON THE DANFORTH ○○
19 LEFT BANK ○○
20 JOSO'S ○○○
21 AVALON ○○○
22 SARKIS ○○
23 LA FENICE ○○○
24 CALIFORNIA SANDWICH ¢
25 INNISKILLIN

26 SPLENDIDO ○○○
27 ATLAS BAR & GRILL ○○
28 FERRO ○
29 THE BOVINE SEX CLUB
30 PETER PAN ○○
31 BAR ITALIA ○○
32 GRAZIE ○
33 606 ○
34 TARO GRILL ○○○
35 THE RIVOLI ○○
36 DUTCH DREAMS ¢
37 PENROSE FISH & CHIPS ¢
38 TERRONI ○
39 THE HORSESHOE TAVERN
40 ED'S WAREHOUSE RESTAURANTS ○
41 JOHN'S ITALIAN CAFFE ○
42 JET FUEL CAFÉ ¢
43 ROSEWATER SUPPER CLUB ○○○
44 LOTUS
45 BOBA ○○○
46 LAKEVIEW LUNCH ¢
47 GYPSY CO-OP ○
48 KALENDAR KOFFEE HOUSE ○
49 ELLIPSIS ○○
50 OPUS ○○○

PRICE BASED ON DINNER FOR TWO WITH WINE ○○○ $100 PLUS ○○ $50–$100 ○ UNDER $50 ¢ ROCK BOTTOM

TOM FEILER

BLACK & BLUE SMOKE BAR

RENAISSANCE PLAZA, 150 BLOOR STREET WEST, TORONTO, CANADA

416 · 920 · 9900

PLATE·1

TOM FEILER

ENOTECA DELLA PIAZZA

150 BLOOR STREET WEST, TORONTO, CANADA

416 · 920 · 9900

ENOTECA
DELLA PIAZZA

PREGO
DELLA PIAZZA

PLATE 2

595 College Street,   Toronto, Canada   416 • 536 • 4564

S O T T O V O C E

RON FEHLING

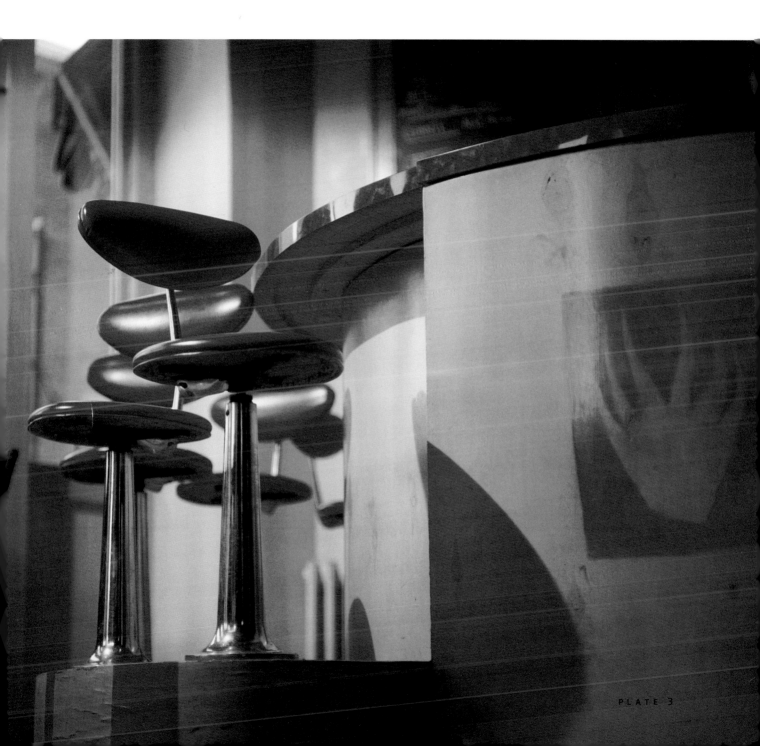

PLATE 3

GEORGE SIMHONI

NORTH 44°

2537 YONGE STREET, TORONTO, CANADA 416 • 487 • 4897

PLATE 4

RON FEHLING

汕頭小食家

S W A T O W R E S T A U R A N T

309 SPADINA AVENUE, TORONTO, CANADA, 416 • 977 • 0601

PLATE 5

ED CHIN

grano

2035 YONGE STREET
TORONTO, CANADA
416 • 440 • 1986

PLATE 6

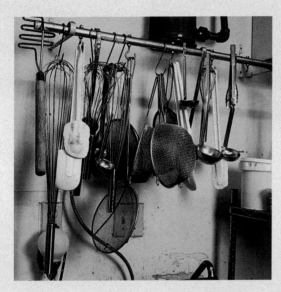

MESSIS

97 HARBORD STREET, TORONTO, CANADA 416 · 920 · 2186

KATHRYN HOLLINRAKE

PLATE 7

FRANK HOEDL

purrr....meow....purrrr....

MENU

297 King Street West, Toronto, Canada   416 • 977 • 4461

PLATE 8

CENTRO

RON FEHLING

2472 YONGE STREET, TORONTO, CANADA 416 • 483 • 2211

PLATE 9

LETTIERI
ESPRESSO BAR - CAFÉ

ED CHIN

LETTIERI, 94 CUMBERLAND STREET, TORONTO, CANADA 416 • 515 • 8764

PLATE 10

GEORGE SIMHONI

canoe

Restaurant and Bar
Fifty Fourth Floor, Toronto Dominion Bank Tower
66 Wellington Street West
Toronto, Canada

416 • 364 • 0054

PLATE 11

ED CHIN

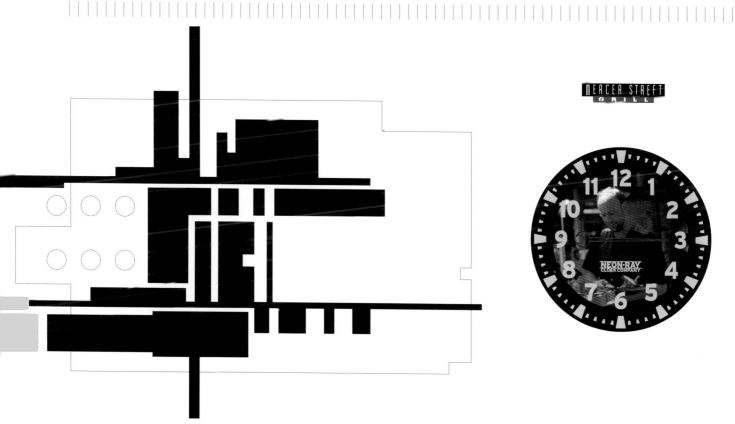

PLATE 12

XANGÔ

A SOUTH AMERICAN BAR AND RESTAURANT

106 JOHN STREET, TORONTO, CANADA

416 · 593 · 4407

PLATE 13

波

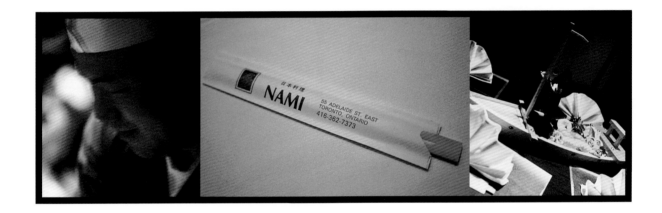

日 本 料 理

NAMI, JAPANESE SEAFOOD RESTAURANT, 55 ADELAIDE STREET EAST, TORONTO, CANADA
416 • 362 • 7373

TOM FEILER

PLATE 14

EIGENSINN FARM, MICHAEL & NOBUYO STADTLÄNDER, R.R. 2, SINGHAMPTON, ONTARIO
519 • 922 • 3128

PLATE 15

FRANK HOEDL

Rodney's Oyster House, 209 Adelaide Street East, Toronto, Canada 416 · 214 · 2877

PLATE 16

IAN CAMPBELL

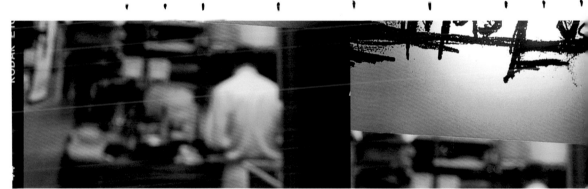

LOLITA'S LUST, 513 DANFORTH AVENUE, TORONTO,CANADA
416 • 465 • 1751

PLATE 17

YOUVE
DONE • IT
ALREADY

PAN ON THE DANFORTH, 516 DANFORTH AVENUE, TORONTO, CANADA 416 • 466 • 8158

ΙΛΕΚ

ANTHONY CHEUNG

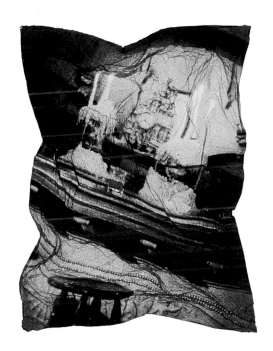

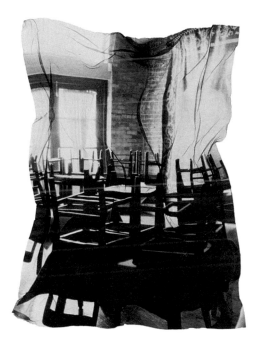

LEFT BANK, 567 QUEEN STREET WEST, TORONTO, CANADA 416 · 504 · 1626

PLATE 19

PLATE 20

KATHRYN HOLLINRAKE

AVALON

270 ADELAIDE STREET WEST, TORONTO, CANADA

416 · 979 · 9918

PLATE 21

 **SARKIS,** 67 RICHMOND STREET EAST, TORONTO, CANADA 416 • 214 • 1337

COUILLARD

TOM FEILER

RON FEHLING

LA FENICE, 319 KING STREET WEST, TORONTO, CANADA 416 • 585 • 2377

PLATE 23

CHRIS GORDANEER

California Sandwiches

244 Claremont Street, Toronto, Canada

416 · 603 · 3317

PLATE 24

Inniskillin

1995 PINOT NOIR RE...

DONALD J.P. ZIRALDO CO-FOUNDER

ORGE SIMHON

PLATE 25

SPLENDIDO, 88 HARBORD STREET, TORONTO, CANADA 416 • 929 • 7788

ED CHIN

PLATE 26

ATLAS
BAR AND GRILL

129 PETER STREET, TORONTO, CANADA 416 · 977 · 7744

TOM FEILER

PLATE 27

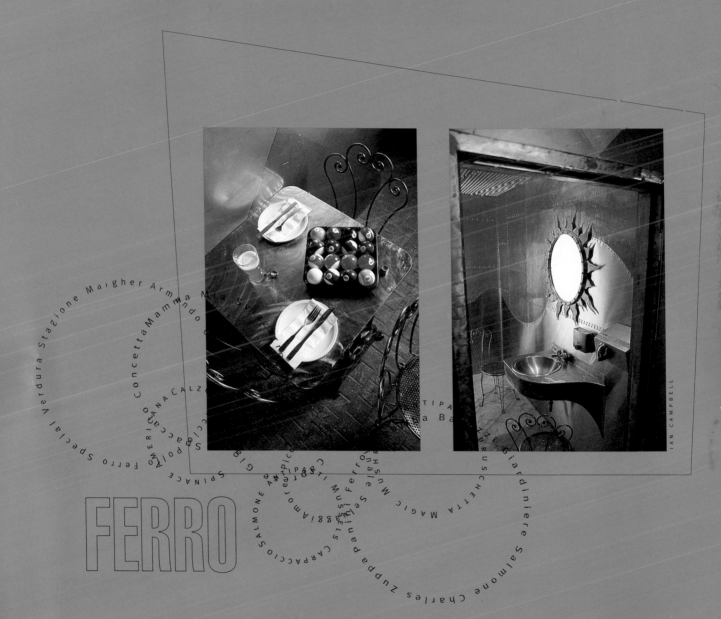

FERRO

IAN CAMPBELL

769 ST. CLAIR AVENUE WEST, TORONTO, CANADA 416 • 654 • 9119

PLATE 28

I have been to the bovine sex club... now I want to go home

chris gordaneer

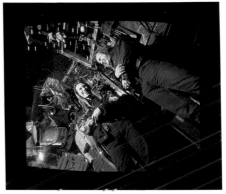

THE **BOVINES EX CLUB** 542 QUEEN STREET WEST Toronto, Canada

WHaddya mean it's past last call ?

5044239

!!!

ECLECTIC MaGical FORMat

ALTER NATIVE ROCK

Celebrity Clientele

EX THE MOO

Eclectic rock, funk techno + *Camp* PLATE 29

pet m
milk m
kill m
eat m

EX CLUB

peter

RON FEHLIN

pan

PETER PAN, 373 QUEEN STREET WEST, TORONTO, CANADA 416 • 593 • 0917

PLATE 30

PANINI
ESPRESSO
BIRRE
PARLARE
SENTIRE
VEDERE

582 COLLEGE STREET
TORONTO, CANADA
416 • 535 • 3621

BAR ITALIA

ANTHONY CHEUNG

PLATE 31

FRANK HOEDL

GRAZIE

GRAZIE RISTORANTE, 2373 YONGE STREET, TORONTO, CANADA 416 • 488 • 0822

PLATE 32

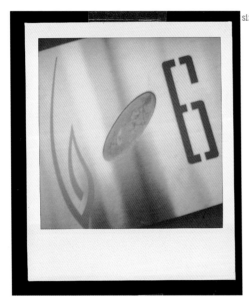

chris gordaneer

6

6°

PLATE 33

RON FELLING

Taro Grill

492 QUEEN STREET WEST, TORONTO, CANADA 416 • 504 • 1320

PLATE 34

Rivoli

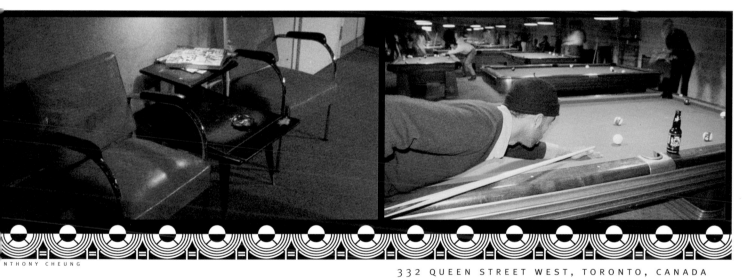

ANTHONY CHEUNG

332 QUEEN STREET WEST, TORONTO, CANADA
416 • 596 • 1908

PLATE 35

Dutch Dreams

78 Vaughan Road
Toronto, Canada
416 * 656 * 6959

PLATE 36

KATHRYN HOL INRAKE

Guest Check

Table no.

Meals

Beverages

Than

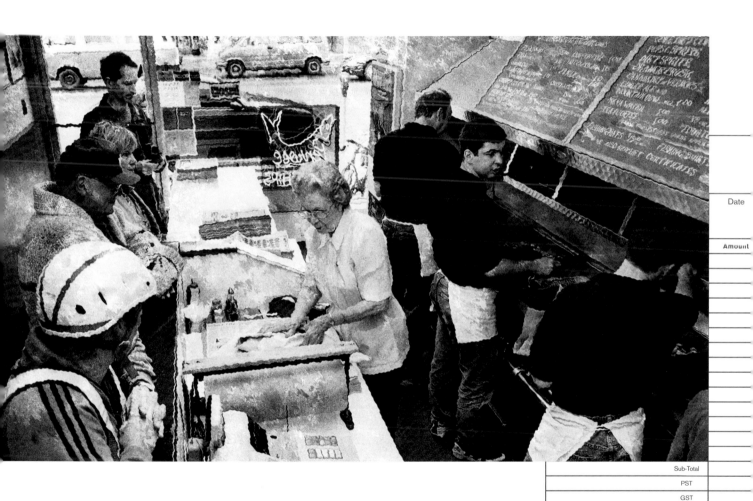

	Date	
	Amount	
Sub-Total		
PST		
GST		
TOTAL		
47481		
Check No.		

Penrose Fish & Chips
600 Mt. Pleasant Road, Toronto, Canada
416 • 483 • 6800

Thank You!

PLATE 37

TERRONI

720 QUEEN STREET WEST, TORONTO, CANADA 416 • 504 • 0320

GEORGE SIMHONI

PLATE 38

PLATE 39

ED'S WAREHOUSE RESTAURANTS, 270 KING STREET WEST, TORORTO, CANADA 416 • 593 • 6676

PLATE 40

pesto *pizza*

masi 93 ruffino   sundried tomatoes roasted pepp...   ...one   amarone del valpolicella.
                   mozzaralla ricotta black olives red pep...   masi 93 ruffino

john's italian caffe
27 baldwin street toronto canada
416 596 8848

PLATE 41

much time drink it up cause you

519 Parliament Street, Toronto, Canada 416 • 968 • 9982

JET FUEL

PLATE 42

IAN CAMPBELL

THE ROSEWATER
SUPPER CLUB

19 TORONTO STEET, TORONTO, CANADA 416 • 214 • 5888

PLATE 43

LOTUS

IAN CAMPBELL

PLATE 44

KATHRYN HOLLINRAKE

boba

90 Avenue Road, Toronto, Canada   416 • 961 • 2622

PLATE 45

Milkshakes

CHOCOLATE
VANILLA
STRAWBERRY
PISTACHIO
BANANA
PINEAPPLE
MALTED
MINT
CAPPUC

LAKEVIEW LUNCH, 1132 DUNDAS STREET WEST, TORONTO, CANADA 416 • 530 • 0871

Gypsy Co-op, 817 Queen Street West, Toronto, Canada 416 • 703 • 5069

RON FEHLING

KALENDAR KOFFEE HOUSE 546 COLLEGE STREET, TORONTO, CANADA   416 • 923 • 4138

PLATE 48

FRANK HOEDL

ellipsis
xxx college street, toronto, canada
416 . 929 . 2892

PLATE 49

7 NIGHTS
M - 2:00AM

RON FEHLI

OPUS

GOOD NIGHT AND THANK YOU VERY MUCH

INDEX

Following is a listing, in alphabetical order, of the places you have just visited. Beat Toronto's intention is to spotlight the range of occasion and potential experience our city has to offer. A traditional rating system has not been used. We have selected what we consider to be terrific examples in a variety of categories, from fine dining to diner. Inclusion constitutes a recommendation. Every effort has been made to ensure that the information is both current and accurate. Unless it is noted, most major credit cards are accepted.

ATLAS BAR & GRILL   **P 27**
129 Peter Street. Eclectic mix of trends in this large multi-level space. The newly revamped kitchen reflects global influences. Intensely popular patio, one of the city's best. Great for people watchers and those who like being watched. Upstairs, the Satellite Lounge blasts off when the stars come out.   416 . 977 . 7544

AVALON   **P 21**
270 Adelaide Street West. Upscale venue for the restrained work of Christopher McDonald. Caters to a diverse mix from both media and corporate worlds. Serene, beautifully appointed room. Mediterranean-edged menu feels the influence of Italy and France. Extensive wine list assembled by the chef.   416 . 979 . 9918

BAR ITALIA P 31

582 College Street. Eugene Barone can be found every night charming the crowds at this new incarnation of the original College Street hangout. Italian-chic decor. Patio out front, espresso bar, booths in the main room make intimate conversations possible. Definitely one for people lovers. 416 . 535 . 3621

BLACK & BLUE P 1

150 Bloor Street West. Tailored, impeccably groomed room heralding the return of the steak after a long, guilty absence. Michael Carlevale again delivers what we have come to expect in this locale at this price point. Smoke bar thoughtfully located upstairs for a well-ventilated cigar. 416 . 920 . 9900

BOBA P 45

90 Avenue Road. Bob Bermann and Barbara Gordon own and operate this cozy upscale gem. Attention to detail ensures a unique and memorable dining experience. The inventive high-end cuisine is the major attraction here. Not afraid to take risks with the wine list. Historic street terrace. 416 . 961 . 2622

THE BOVINE SEX CLUB P29

542 Queen Street West. Coiled on Queen Street for 5 years, Toronto's answer to the Viper Room. The leather-clad denizens as distinctive as the Dada-garbage decor. Pool tables out back, off-beat film and video out front. Heavy rock. Sunday brunch with mom? Maybe not. 416 . 504 . 4239

CALIFORNIA SANDWICHES P 24

244 Claremont Street. You'll find all types from corporates to construction workers on line here. Veal sandwiches are definitely the star item. Speedy, efficient service from the friendly all female staff keeps the crowd moving. Couldn't be fresher, better or cheaper. Mama mia. 416 . 603 . 3317

CANOE P 11

66 Wellington Street West. The room at the top. Fifty four floors above the traffic Michael Bonacini and Peter Oliver stroke the Brooks Brothers crowd you would expect to find in a bank tower. An inventive Canadian-themed menu from chefs Todd Clarmo and Anthony Walsh. Discerning wine list. 416 . 364 . 0054

CENTRO P 9

2472 Yonge Street. Marc Thuet's culinary flair with Canadian ingredients combined with Tony Longo's front of house polish ensure Centro's continued dominance of Toronto's top end. Dressy, expensive, an occasion for most, hard for some to imagine lifestyles that include this on a regular basis. 416 . 483 . 2211

DUTCH DREAMS P 36

78 Vaughan Road. Ever wondered at the line-up curling around this riotously decorated building just north of St. Clair West? In 1985 father and son Theo and Theo Aben opened Dutch Dreams. Indulge every fantasy, (childhood or otherwise), around frozen desserts. Have to see it to believe it. 416 . 656 . 6959

ED'S WAREHOUSE RESTAURANTS P 40

270 King Street West. "Honest Ed Mirvish", a name synonymous with civic pride created Ed's Warehouse one year after his purchase and renovation of the the Royal Alexandra Theatre. Old Ed's and Ed's Seafood followed. "Good basic food and good value". Opulent, fantastic, antique-filled decor. 416 . 593 . 6676

EIGENSINN FARM P 15

RR #2 Singhampton, Ontario. Truly more than a meal. Michael Stadtländer, responsible for much of Toronto's culinary evolution, provides a dining experience combining the freshest country harvest with an escape from the city. No credit or cellar so bring your own wine and plenty of cash. 519 . 821 . 2852

ELLIPSIS P 49

503 College Street. Nancy Barone's newest venture on the restaurant-laden College West strip. Foodies have rapidly spread the word and Ellipsis is packed. Perfect spot for brunch if you don't mind the wait. Breads and pastries are baked on the premises. All food is organic. Unusual blonde decor. 416 . 929 . 2892

ENOTECA DELLA PIAZZA, PREGO P 2

150 Bloor Street West. Michael Carlevale and Massimo Capra create the rooms one would expect in the hub of chic Toronto. One of the best spots for stargazing in Hollywood North. Capra's kitchen is consistently terrific. Top notch wines. Live piano a classy alternative to musak. 416 . 920 . 9900

FERRO   **P 28**

769 St. Clair Avenue West. Frank, Armando, and Carmen Pronesti show that the second generation still has something fresh to offer Little Italy. A hugely popular neighbourhood hangout with emphasis on authentic Italian menu favourites. Big portions, small prices, one of a kind decor.   416 . 654 . 9119

GRANO   **P 6**

2035 Yonge Street. The first truly successful restaurant on the stretch of Yonge between Davisville and Eglinton. Roberto and Lucia Martella's family affair serves a huge selection of antipasti, pizzas, and daily specials. Lovely garden patio tucked outback. Complete take-out and catering service.   416 . 440 . 1986

GYPSY CO-OP   **P 47**

817 Queen Street West. This recent arrival on Queen Street's hip strip is a patchwork of unlikely ingredients—general store, lounge, bar, news agent, and the best of surprises, excellent food. Heavy on the organics. Artsy staff. The Borg brothers lay down a good vibe. Peace.   416 . 703 . 5069

GRAZIE   **P 32**

2373 Yonge Street. Lively, crowded spot for locals who don't always want to make the trek downtown. You're made to feel a part of this family owned and operated venue. Gourmet pizzas and pasta dominate. No reservations, but the high energy staff moves the crowds efficiently in and out.   416 . 488 . 0822

THE HORSESHOE TAVERN   **P 39**

368 Queen Street West. The denim jeans of Toronto bars—and that's black denim. Fifty years of the best scene around. Live music in the back room ranges from the sublime to bad Stones' covers. If you ain't had a signifi-cant night at the 'Shoe then you're not livin' in the city.   416 . 598 . 4753

INNISKILLIN VINEYARDS   **P 25**

Niagara-on-the-Lake, Service Road 6, RR 1, Niagara Parkway at line 3, Ontario. Canadian wines are earning international acclaim and Inniskillin is largely responsible, most notably with Icewine. Escape the city for a memorable day and a tour of the vineyard with host and co-founder Donald Ziraldo.   905 . 468 . 3554

JET FUEL CAFÉ   **P 42**

519 Parliament Street. The bike boys with caf-feinated bloodstreams get their transfusions at this funky Cabbagetown pit stop. Easy going staff lays back while the clientele gears up. Rocket bottom prices. The Jet Fuel, one pint in size, plus biscotti can be had for a twoonie. Beat that.   416 . 968 . 9982

JOHN'S ITALIAN CAFFE   **P 41**

27 Baldwin Street. A simple devotion to all things Italian characterizes this cozy unpre-tentious, haven on Baldwin. Renown for its pizza, friendly, casual service, and moderate pricing John's is a favourite among students and the artistically inclined. Family-oriented and attitude-free.   416 . 596 . 8848

JOSO'S   **P 20**

202 Davenport Road. A family-run restaurant where the family are all artists. Joso Spralja, a founding member of Toronto's bohemia, has provided a careful dedication to seafood for 20 years. Toronto's best calamari. Favourite with visiting celebs. Decor? What can one say that hasn't been said already . . .   416 . 925 . 1903

KALENDAR KOFFEE HOUSE   **P 48**

546 College Street. Tiny, oak-paneled space inherits some of its decor from old churches. Owners are responsible for the fabulous mirrors and light fixtures. The menu, an inventive mix of salads, pastas and sandwiches. Wide selection of beers, ciders and coffees. Desserts suit the really sweet of tooth.   416 . 923 . 4138

KIT KAT   **P 8**

297 King Street. Al Carbone's New York style eatery is a perfect fit for the entertainment district. Home style, Southern Italian cuisine. Jam-packed skinny front room wraps around a tree (honest) and opens up out back. The friendly, welcoming staff makes it impossible to feel lonely here.   416 . 977 . 4461

LA FENICE   **P 23**

319 King Street West. Located in the heart of the financial and entertainment districts, La Fenice has held the power crowd for fifteen years. A beautifully appointed room, flawless Italian cuisine, and a top notch wine list are responsible for a full house both at noon and at night.   416 . 585 . 2377

LAKEVIEW LUNCH P 46

1132 Dundas Street West. Now in its 50th year this authentically appointed diner is everything you would hope. Traditions are respected in the kitchen as well, from the all day breakfast to burgers and the milkshakes in stainless containers. Best of all, you really have to work to spend over ten dollars here. 416 . 530 . 0871

LEFT BANK P 19

567 Queen Street West. Serious, imposing gothic decor is matched by serious cuisine. Nothing quite like it in the city. Very crowded bar, worth it for the caesars. Pool tables are clad in unexpected colours. May seem familiar from the many times it has provided backdrop for a video or film. 416 . 504 . 1626

LETTIERI P 10

94 Cumberland Street. Fueling Toronto's love affair with the bean, Lettieri creates greater ambience than the franchised coffee shops. Grilled panini, pizza and salads provide more than the usual sugary snack to accompany your fix. Staff pours on the Italian charm at six locations. 416 . 515 . 8764

LOLITA'S LUST P 17

513 Danforth Avenue. Behind a painted green window, Queen Street meets the Danforth. Updated Mediterranean cuisine in an amusing deconstructivist decor. Side dishes are à la carte, giving you greater control over your meal. Lolita's mixes a martini that justifies the current cocktail mania. 416 . 465 . 1751

LOTUS P 44

As Beat Toronto went to press, the rumours that have long surrounded Susur Lee came to ground with the closure of the legendary Tecumseth Street location. Lee is a major contributor to our city's world wide culinary stature. Although no longer a part of Toronto's future, Lotus remains a cherished piece of our past.

MERCER STREET GRILL P 12

36 Mercer Street. An elegant, architecturally disciplined decor in this strict modern space. Owned and run by Simon Bower. Sophisticated, Southeast Asian inspired menu under the careful direction of Chef Renée Foote. The Japanese garden patio, a recent addition, moves it all outside in the summertime. 416 . 599 . 3399

MESSIS P 7

97 Harbord Street. Eugene Shewchuk creates artfully presented dishes that rise up off the plate to meet you. Wine list is both carefully selected and well priced. Comfortable and casual atmosphere. One of Toronto's loveliest patios for those precious few days we can dine outside. 416 . 920 . 2186

NAMI P 14

55 Adelaide Street East. Serene, classically Japanese room situated in the city's business district is a haven for sushi lovers. Discreet, private booths. Tatami room for larger parties. Gentle-mannered servers counterpoint the high energy performance on display in the open kitchen. 416 . 362 . 7373

NORTH 44° P 4

2537 Yonge Street. Mark McEwan's entry at Toronto's high end. Always innovative in the kitchen with a concentration on cross-cultural combinations. Airy decor only rivaled by the spectacular food presentation. Excellent wine list given special status by The Wine Spectator in 1996. 416 . 487 . 4897

OPUS P 50

37 Prince Arthur Avenue. One of the power rooms, witness to some serious deal making. Superlative wine list, accredited by The Wine Spectator. Attentive service by the Amaro brothers and their smooth staff. Sophisticated haute cuisine by Paul Boehmer, one of our most talented young chefs. 416 . 921 . 3105

PAN ON THE DANFORTH P 18

516 Danforth Avenue. Johnny K's version of upscale on the Danforth. In the centre of one of Toronto's most renown villages, Chef Laura Prentice acknowledges the cultural traditions of the neighbourhood while updating the Greek-fusion menu with some contemporary twists. 416 . 466 . 8158

PENROSE FISH AND CHIPS P 37

600 Mt. Pleasant Road. Ever since 1950 the Johnstons have been fishin' and frying fresh halibut in batter that's a secret family recipe. That's a long time to keep a secret. Chunky-cut fries and a newspaper wrapping complete a meal you may have thought extinct. Can't catch them in July. 416 . 483 . 6800

PETER PAN — P 30

373 Queen Street West. A landmark in the evolution of the Queen Street strip, Peter Pan was here long before anyone else cashed in. Thirties diner decor carefully preserved, most notably the coveted booths. Cozy tables by the large bay windows in front. Intimate patio. Rotating art shows on the walls.　416 . 593 . 0917

THE RIVOLI — P 35

332 Queen Street West. Quintessential Queen Street. The Riv gives you the chance to shoot some pool over a few, catch a live band that may be huge in a years' time, experience Thai-driven cuisine in the somber main room or eyeball the Q West parade from perhaps the best patio on the strip.　416 . 596 . 1908

RODNEY'S OYSTER HOUSE — P 16

209 Adelaide Street East. Boisterous, offbeat, underground space full of high-octane staff and the freshest bivalves around. Rodney's is tops for entertainment and value. Although the place has little visibility from the street the crowds have managed to find it. Memorable and unique.　416 . 363 . 8105

ROSEWATER SUPPER CLUB — P 43

19 Toronto Street. The decor is designed to impress in this renovated historic venue. The Asian-continental cuisine, a fusion of old and new influences. Bar in front usually packed with the Bay Street crowd. Downstairs, a room for private functions and a lounge for that fashionable cigar.　416 .214 . 5888

SARKIS — P 22

67 Richmond Street East. Greg Couillard makes another appearance on our culinary landscape in this small space named for its owner, Sarkis. All notoriety can be forgiven when the plate meets the table. A wizard with spices and surprising combinations, each dish an almost erotic thrill.　416 . 214 . 1337

SOTTO VOCE — P 3

595 College Street. Scion of Giancarlo's this tiny, sleek wine bar with food perched on the restaurant-intensive stretch of College, is a natural setting for the heavily art directed. Night hawks keep the room lively right up to last call. Chalk boards announce varied wines by the glass.　416 . 536 . 4564

SPLENDIDO — P 26

88 Harbord Street. Arpi Magyar, master of both kitchen and dining room, is the heart and soul of this permanently popular Harbord Street beauty. Thoroughly professional staff, top notch food, wine and the tremendous desserts make it hard to go wrong here. Always an occasion.　416 . 929 . 7788

SWATOW — P 5

309 Spadina Avenue. Located on a stretch of Spadina thick with Asian late nights, Swatow is consistently packed. Waiters navigate the mirrored room with a speed geared to the sizzling Cantonese dishes. Heavy traffic after last call. Open till 5 a.m. Stop at the bank machine first, as it's cash only.　416 . 977 . 0601

TARO GRILL — P 34

492 Queen Street West. Owners Scott Kerr and Stephen Gardner create a cozy, stylish room low on attitude, high on spirit. Perfect for a bite with a friend you haven't seen in ages. Generous servings, moderate prices. Booths for intimacy, tiny patio, friendly bar and a great brunch too.　416 . 504 . 1720

TERRONI — P 38

720 Queen Street West. Packed with patrons and atmosphere this tiny diner is a strong contender for the city's best panino and pizza. Easy to find other favourites on the menu. Don't miss dessert. Small selection of imported Italian foodstuffs. Take-out and catering. Very friendly prices, cash only.　416 . 504 . 0320

XANGÔ — P 13

106 John Street. Nuevo Latino cuisine in an appropriately Latin decor. It's one of the few spots in town for lovers of South American spices. Detailed, extensive menu features a glossary to inform and enlighten. The live and lively music has them dancing in the aisles on weekends.　416 . 593 . 4407

606 — P 39

606 King Street West. A constant choice of the film set, 606 sees lots of wrap parties. Spacious pool room in back. In front, original garage doors roll up and bring the outside inside. High quality, inexpensive fare served up by a very good looking staff. Plenty of bar action too.　416 . 504 . 8740

GEORGE SIMHONI WESTSIDE STUDIO 416 • 535 • 1955

CHRIS GORDANEER WESTSIDE STUDIO 416 • 535 • 1955

IAN CAMPBELL WESTSIDE STUDIO 416 • 535 • 1955

TOM FEILER WESTSIDE STUDIO 416 • 535 • 1955

SAY CHEESE

Here are the artists responsible for the images. Working at times in tight spaces, dim light and a few hours, they demonstrated creative professionalism, a humour, and grace for which we are eternally indebted. Without their efforts this book simply would not exist.

ED CHIN   416 • 716 • 6697

RON FEHLING WESTSIDE STUDIO   416 • 535 • 1955

FRANK HOEDL WESTSIDE STUDIO   416 • 535 • 1955

ANTHONY CHEUNG WESTSIDE STUDIO   416 • 535 • 1955

KATHRYN HOLLINRAKE   416 • 465 • 8280

WE WOULD LIKE TO EXTEND A HEARTFELT THANK YOU TO OUR SPONSORS FOR THEIR GENEROSITY AND VISION